Planes

Chris Oxlade

Heinemann Library
Chicago, Illinois

v WM

Published by Heinemann Library, an imprint of Reed Educational & Professional Publishing,
100 N. LaSalle, Suite 1010
Customer Service 888–454–2279
Visit our website at www.heinemannlibrary.com

Designed by Paul Davies and Associates
Originated by Ambassador Litho
Printed in Hong Kong, China

05 04 03 02 01
10 9 8 7 6 5 4 3 2 1

Library of Congress Catalog-in- Publication Data
Oxlade, Chris.
     Planes / Chris Oxlade.
          p. cm. – (Transportation around the world)
     Includes bibliographical references and index.
     Summary: Brief text and photographs explain what planes are, describe different types of planes, and examine how they developed and how they are used.
     ISBN 1-57572-303-4
     1. Airplanes—Juvenile literature. [1. Airplanes.] I. Title. II. Series.
TL547.O95423 2000
629.133'34—dc21

00-027549

Acknowledgments
The publisher would like to thank the following for permission to reproduce photographs:
Corbis/George Hall, p. 21; Vince Streano, p. 25; Photodisc, pp. 23, 29; Quadrant Picture Library/Jeremy Hoare, pp. 5, 13; R. Shaw, p. 7; Flight, pp. 6, 8, 9, 11, 20, 26; Erik Simonsen, p. 12; Trent Jones, p. 15; Mark Wagner, p. 16; LG Photo, p.17; Anthony R. Dalton, p. 18; Paul Phelan, p. 19; Tony Hobbs, pp. 22, 24, 27; The Stock Market/Russell Munson, p. 10; Tony Stone Images/Alan Smith, p. 14; World Perspectives, p. 28; Trip/Malcolm Fife, p. 4.

Cover photo: Tony Stone
Every effort has been made to contact copyright holders of any material reproduced in this book. Any omissions will be rectified in subsequent printings if notice is given to the publisher.

Note to the Reader
Some words are shown in bold, **like this.**
You can find out what they mean by looking in the glossary.

Contents

What Is a Plane?

A plane is a machine that flies through the air. Some planes carry passengers. Some planes carry **goods**, or cargo. Some people fly planes for fun.

The person who flies a plane is called the **pilot**. The pilot controls the take-off and landing, and **steers** the plane through the air. Some pilots have computers to help them fly the plane.

How Planes Work

Wings keep a plane in the air. As the plane flies, some air rushes under the wings, and some air rushes over the wings. The air pushes the wings upward.

6

Engines give a plane the power to fly. An engine makes the **propeller** spin. The propeller **blades** push air backward, which makes the plane go forward.

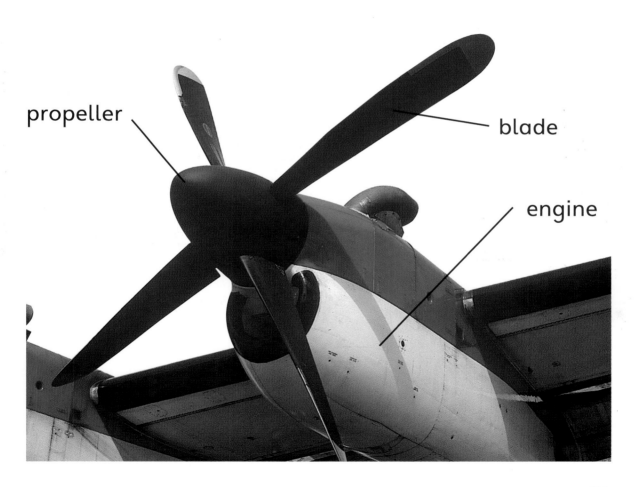

propeller

blade

engine

Planes in the Past

This plane was called *Flyer 1*. It was the first plane to fly using an **engine**. It was built in 1903 by two American brothers, Orville and Wilbur Wright.

An **airliner** is a plane that carries passengers. This is what one of the first airliners looked like. It was slow and very noisy. This plane has two sets of wings.

Where Are Planes Used?

Planes are used all over the world. Almost every country in the world can be reached by airplanes. Jet **airliners** carry people and cargo too.

People get on and off planes at an airport. This is a busy place where many planes take off and land. Planes take off and land on a **runway**.

Airliners

Passenger planes are called **airliners**. The Boeing 747 is the biggest airliner in the world. It is sometimes called a jumbo jet.

More than 500 people can sit inside a jumbo jet. During the flight, the passengers eat a meal and can watch a movie. Jumbo jets fly on long journeys all over the world.

Supersonic Planes

Supersonic planes fly faster than sound. Most supersonic planes are used in the military. Concorde is the only supersonic **airliner**. It carries passengers to places all over the world very quickly.

Concorde has a long, pointed nose. When Concorde is ready to land, the nose drops down so that the **pilot** can see the **runway** ahead.

Cargo Planes

A cargo plane carries **goods,** or cargo. Inside the plane is a cargo **hold**. Boxes are tied down to keep them from moving around during the flight.

A cargo plane has a big door that opens wide. Then large pieces of cargo can be placed in the plane. A special truck lifts the cargo up to the door.

Seaplanes

A seaplane takes off and lands on water. Seaplanes are useful in places where there is plenty of water and nowhere to build a **runway**.

Floats let the seaplane glide across the water for take-offs and landings. Some places in the world are far from cities and roads. People must use seaplanes to get to these places.

Jump Jets

Some planes, such as the Harrier jet, can take off by flying straight up into the air instead of using a **runway**. The Harrier can also fly like a normal plane.

Jump jets can be
used by armies when
runways can't be built.
Jump jets can also land
on ships on water or in
crowded city areas.

21

Gliders

A glider is a plane without an **engine**. A glider has long, thin wings. The wings keep the glider up as it flies slowly. People fly gliders for fun and sport.

A glider is towed into the air by another plane. Gliders then glide slowly back to the ground. The glider's smooth shape lets it cut easily through the air.

Ultralights

This tiny plane is called an ultralight. It can only carry one or two people. People throughout the world fly ultralights for fun.

The **pilot's** seat hangs underneath the wing. The pilot **steers** the plane up and down, and to the left and right, by moving a bar that is attached to the wing.

Jet Fighters

Military planes are used in wars to fight other planes in the air. They also attack targets on the ground. Fighters are small, fast planes that can turn very quickly.

Fighters attack enemy planes with **missiles** and guns. The missiles hang under the fighter's wings. To fire a missile, the **pilot** presses a button in the **cockpit**.

Space Planes

The space shuttle is a plane that goes into space. It takes off like a rocket. Booster rockets give it an extra push.

parachute

When its job in space is finished, the shuttle returns to Earth. It glides down and lands on a **runway** like a regular plane. Parachutes help it to slow down.

29

Important Dates

1783 A hot-air balloon made by the Montgolfier brothers in France carries people into the air for the first time.

1852 The first **airship** takes off in France with its builder, Henry Giffard, aboard.

1903 In the United States, the Wright brothers take off in their airplane, *Flyer 1*. It is the first airplane with an **engine** to fly.

1933 American **pilot** Wiley Post flies around the world on his own. The 15,525-mile (25,000-kilometer) flight takes almost eight days.

1969 The first Boeing 747 jumbo jet takes off for a test flight. Passengers first flew in a 747 in 1970.

1969 In France, the supersonic **airliner** Concorde flies for the first time. It starts carrying passengers in 1976.

1981 The space shuttle *Columbia* takes off for the first time from the Kennedy Space Center in Florida. It **orbits** Earth and then glides down again.

Glossary

airliner	large plane that carries passengers
airship	balloon with an engine that makes it move
blade	one of the long, flat pieces of a propeller
cockpit	place in a plane where the pilot sits
engine	machine that makes the plane move
hold	part of the plane where goods and luggage are kept
goods	things that people buy and sell
jet	type of engine that sends a stream of gas backward that pushes the plane forward
missile	object that flies straight through the air and explodes when it reaches its target
orbit	to travel around an object
pilot	person who flies the plane
propeller	part of plane that spins to make the plane move
runway	long, straight strip of ground where planes take off and land
steers	guides the direction of the plane

Index

More Books to Read

Fradin, Dennis B. *Airplanes*. Danbury, Conn.: Children's Press, 1997.

Schaefer, Lola. *Airplanes*. Mankato, Minn.: Capstone Press, 1999.

Thompson, C.E. *How Do Airplanes Fly?*. New York: Scholastic, 1997.